VERSUS!

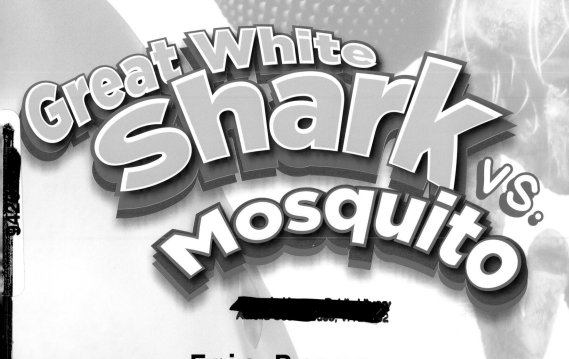

Great White Shark vs. Mosquito

Eric Braun

BLACK
RABBIT
BOOKS

Hi Jinx is published by Black Rabbit Books
P.O. Box 3263, Mankato, Minnesota, 56002.
www.blackrabbitbooks.com
Copyright © 2018 Black Rabbit Books

Marysa Storm & Jennifer Besel, editors; Michael Sellner,
designer; Grant Gould & Catherine Cates, production
designers; Omay Ayres, photo researcher

Library of Congress Cataloging-in-Publication Data
Title: Great white shark vs. mosquito / by Eric Braun.
Other titles: Great white shark versus mosquito
Description: Mankato, Minnesota : Black Rabbit Books, [2018] | Series:
Hi jinx. Versus! | Audience: Ages 9-12. | Audience: Grades 4 to 6. | Includes
bibliographical references and index.
Identifiers: LCCN 2017009990 (print) | LCCN 2017021636 (ebook) |
ISBN 9781680723793 (e-book) | ISBN 9781680723496 (library binding) |
ISBN 9781680726558 (paperback)
Subjects: LCSH: White shark--Juvenile literature. | Mosquitoes--Juvenile
literature. | Animals--Miscellanea--Juvenile literature.
Classification: LCC QL638.95.L3 (ebook) | LCC QL638.95.L3 B73 2018 (print) |
DDC 590.2--dc23
LC record available at https://lccn.loc.gov/2017009990

Printed in China. 9/17

Image Credits

Alamy: Jeff Rotman, 3 (eye); bbls5.rssing.com, 20 (camera); Dreamstime:
Andreykuzmin, 4 (shark); iStock: -asi, Cover, 4 (shark); clairevis, 6 (shark);
memoangeles, 18 (mosquito); Shutterstock: anfisa focusova, 16 (bkgd);
Auspicious, 21 (mosquito); Budi Susanto_awan design, 16 (mosquito); Catmando,
1 (l); Christos Georghiou, 4 (paper); Cornel Constantin, 1 (r); designer_an, 12,
21 (bkgd); Dolimac, 19 (shark); Dusan Pavlic, 11 (kid); Elenarts, 2–3 (teeth);
FebrianGraves, Cover, 5 (mosquito); frescomovie, Back Cover, Cover (bkgd);
GraphicsRF, 8 (shark), 20 (shark); Ilya Chalyuk, 5, 6, 18, 20 (marker); Jeff
Cameron Collingwood, 15 (shark); Julien Tromeur, 13; Liusa, 8 (bl), 12
(shark); Memo Angeles, 12 (blue fish); millerium arkay, 7 (coin); monoo, 6
(kids); opicobello, 7 (paper tear), 8 (marker), 11 (paper tear); owatta,
18-19 (ring); Pakso Maksim, Back Cover, 17, 23, 24 (paper tear);
Pitju, 21 (paper); Pylypchuk, 6–7 (bus); Refluo, 14 (mosquito);
Sujono sujono, 7 (mosquito); Teguh Mujiono, 10–11
(mosquitos), 14-15 (sea and seals); Top Vector Studios,
11 (mosquito); totallypic, 6-7, 18-19 (arrows); Trexyca, 8
(br), 23; Tueris, Cover (marker); vitasunny, 12
(green fish)

Contents

4

Chapter 1
Deadly Bites

Great white sharks have grins full of sharp teeth. They are also huge animals. Mosquitoes are tiny. Their bites aren't painful. But these little critters can carry deadly diseases. What would happen if we put these two animals in a fight?

Chapter 2
Comparing Their Features

Female great whites are often bigger than males. They grow more than 20 feet (6 meters) long. How long is that? It's about half a school bus.

Mosquitoes, on the other hand, aren't so big. They are only up to .75 inch (2 centimeters) long. That's as long as a penny.

Weight

Most mosquitoes weigh .000005 pound (.000002 kilogram). That's why you don't notice them land on you. One jelly bean weighs as much as 567 mosquitoes.

You'd definitely notice a great white landing on you! They weigh about 5,000 pounds (2,268 kg)! That's about 2 million jelly beans.

Speed

Great whites can swim up to 35 miles (56 kilometers) per hour. But that's only for short bursts. They usually swim much slower than that.

Mosquitoes fly about 1.2 miles (2 km) per hour. You can run faster than that. But these insects are quick. They **dodge** swatting hands. They fly through small spaces too. You can run, but you can't hide.

Mosquitoes beat their wings about 600 times per second.

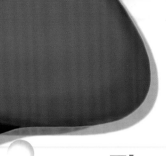

The Bite

Can you imagine staring into the mouth of a great white? They have about 300 triangle-shaped teeth. The edges are rough. They're just like saw blades. The teeth are made for tearing.

A mosquito doesn't have teeth. Instead, it has a **proboscis**. It's like a built-in straw. And a mosquito's **victim** is like one big juice box. The insect stabs the **prey** with the tube. Then it drinks.

proboscis

On the Hunt

Great whites are dark on top. They blend in with the ocean bottom. They wait until seals or sea lions swim above them. Then they dart up. The sharks **ram** into their prey. They bite at the same time.

Only female mosquitoes are out for blood. They use their sense of smell to hunt. Scientists believe they can sense breathing from 164 feet (50 m) away. They zero in and fly to their target. Then they begin to feed.

Chapter 3
Who Would Win?

Great whites and mosquitoes
are both deadly creatures.
Who would win?

Mosquitoes are
quick and quiet.

They have a strong
sense of smell.

They can carry
deadly diseases.

Secret Weapon

Sharks have a special power. Animals make small electric fields. Sharks can sense them. This **ability** helps them track prey.

Mosquitoes' secret weapons are the diseases they can carry. The insects pass on diseases when they feed. One of the worst is malaria. This disease kills thousands of people every year.

Great white sharks kill fewer than 15 people every year. Germs in mosquito bites kill about 725,000 people each year.

Great whites have rows of sharp teeth.

They can swim up to 35 miles (56 km) per hour.

They are built to hunt.

19

Chapter 4
Get in on the Hi Jinx

Great whites are difficult to study. They spend most of their time deep underwater. Scientists don't know where they go. In 2013, scientists put a robot to work. They attached a SharkCam to the bot. Then they sent it into the ocean.

In the dark depths, the bot recorded sharks' behaviors. Sometimes the sharks bumped the bot. Other times, they bit it. The information recorded told scientists more about sharks.

Take It One Step More

1. Mosquitoes are dangerous. Should people get rid of them? Why or why not?

2. Shark attacks are rare. But many people are still afraid of sharks. Why do you think that is?

3. What do great white sharks and mosquitoes have in common?

GLOSSARY

ability (uh-BI-luh-tee)—the power or skill to do something

dodge (DAHDJ)—to move quickly in order to avoid being hit

prey (PRAY)—an animal hunted or killed for food

proboscis (prah-BAH-sis)—a long, thin tube that forms part of the mouth of some insects

ram (RAM)—to strike with violence

victim (VIK-tim)—someone or something injured or killed

BOOKS

Hunt, Santana. *Bloodsucking Mosquitoes.* Real-Life Vampires. New York: Gareth Stevens Publishing, 2016.

Pettiford, Rebecca. *Great White Sharks.* Ocean Life Up Close. Minneapolis: Bellwether Media, 2017.

Waxman, Laura Hamilton. *Great White Sharks.* Sharks. Mankato, MN: Amicus High Interest, Amicus Ink, 2017.

WEBSITES

Great White Shark
animals.nationalgeographic.com/animals/fish/great-white-shark/

Great White Shark
www.bbc.co.uk/programmes/articles/22PvxQxZX9NTdgZrCnX0S0f/great-white-shark

Mosquito
kids.nationalgeographic.com/animals/mosquito/#mosquito-closeup.jpg

INDEX